Table of Contents

I0448616

Introduction

The war in Afghanistan recently passed the ten-year milestone with much more work still ahead. Over the years as the insurgency began to flourish, the International Security Assistance Force (ISAF) and the U.S. Government (USG) adopted a comprehensive campaign to counteract the insurgent's influence on the population. This campaign plan includes three lines of effort; Security, Governance and Reconstruction and Development.[1] As the major contributing nation to NATO and ISAF, The United States has formulated a detailed strategy to align with these three lines of effort contributing billions of dollars along the way. The USG's aims within the Governance and Reconstruction and Development lines of effort are to develop the local economies and foster a free and democratic form of government. There are many initiatives, which fit into these lines of effort. For example, Agricultural Development Teams (ADTs) introduce new farming techniques and alternative crops to Afghan farmers in an effort to increase productivity, income and reduce poppy cultivation. The Commander's Emergency Response Program (CERP) provides money to operational commanders for development projects in their operational areas, which enables local governance. The USG has organized and fielded Provincial Reconstruction Teams (PRTs) to foster good governance and help develop infrastructure. In spite of all this effort, some evidence suggests that the Afghan people are not using these programs and the facilities and infrastructure they create.[2] This is puzzling to many westerners who do not understand why Afghans reject these ideas and programs that seem to have obvious benefits. If Afghans do not adopt these programs, then the USG's efforts are fruitless. Thus, the USG would benefit greatly from an analysis as to how it can adjust or tailor its programs to encourage increased adoption.

Fortunately, a large body of academic work exists that examines this very phenomenon, the diffusion of innovations. Diffusion research, first presented in 1962 by Everett M. Rogers in his book by

---

[1] International Security Assistance Force, Afghanistan "About ISAF" 2011. NATO, http://www.isaf.nato.int/mission.html (accessed 25 October 2011).

[2] Lorraine Sherman *Sustainability of US Government Projects in Afghanistan* (Mongraph, School of Advanced Military Studies, Command and General Staff College, Fort Leavenworth, KS, 2011), 1.

the same title, provides a solid and generally accepted framework for understanding how innovations (ideas and technology) diffuse across (or are adopted by) a social system.[3] Rogers posits that the attributes of an innovation as perceived by the social system are key indicators of its rate of adoption. These attributes include; the *relative advantage* of the innovation, the *compatibility* of the innovation with the social system (culture), the *complexity* of the innovation, the ability to use the innovation on a trial basis (*trialability*) and the ability of the people to see the positive results of an innovation (*observability*).[4] While Rogers was not the first person to do diffusion research, he was the first person to conceptualize the diffusion of innovations theory into a comprehensive body of work. His elements of diffusion of innovations and his model have gained wide acceptance in the communication, and sociology disciplines. In fact, many researchers have used diffusion of innovations to analyze and explain social phenomenon closely related to the kinds of ideas the USG is currently promoting and working to diffuse in Afghanistan.

This work applies the diffusion of innovations theory and model in the analysis of the USG's governance and development efforts in Afghanistan to determine if the key elements of diffusion of innovations are present. Furthermore, this monograph seeks to determine if these elements, when present, correlate with the Afghans' increased adoption of the programs. Where the elements of diffusion of innovations are found in USG governance and development efforts, those efforts should be more successful. While many nations contribute to the ISAF mission along these two crucial lines of effort, this work will focus on only the USG's programs in order to limit the analysis to a manageable level. However, the author contends that if the research were expanded and similar analysis conducted on any governance or development endeavor in Afghanistan the same correlations would be found.

---

[3] Everett M. Rogers, *Diffusion of Innovations*, 5th ed. (New York: Free Press, 2003), 23. Rogers defines social system as "a set of interrelated units (individuals) that are engaged in joint problem solving to accomplish a common goal" This term is more fully explained in a latter section of this monograph.

[4] Ibid. 15-16.

This work will first examine the literature concerning diffusion of innovations. The rest of the monograph is organized utilizing three of the four elements of diffusion of innovations; social system, communication channel and the innovation. Then the work examines development and governance initiatives using five attributes of an innovation if they apply.

Diffusion of Innovations: A Review of the Literature

If we acknowledge that the governance and development lines of effort involve ideas that the USG is trying to persuade Afghans to adopt, then an application of knowledge obtained through diffusion research would be helpful in analyzing these programs to determine how the USG can improve and accelerate the adoption process. Therefore, an understanding of the theory of diffusion of innovations is necessary.

Although scholars may not have called it diffusion of innovations, many had been doing diffusion-based research for a considerable time before Rogers' 1962 book. Over the decades, the theory has gained wide acceptance in the communication, and sociology disciplines. Many researchers have used diffusion of innovations to analyze and explain social phenomenon closely related to the kinds of ideas the United States is currently promoting and working to diffuse in Afghanistan. For example, scholars in rural sociology, Bryce Ryan and Neil Gross examined the adoption of hybrid corn seed by Iowa Farmers in the early 1940s.[5] David Belasco, in his Ph. D dissertation, examined the reasons the practice of purifying drinking water in Egyptian villages failed to diffuse across that society.[6]

Diffusion of innovations research evolved and expanded out of several research traditions almost simultaneously, but largely independently.[7] Some of the major disciplines in which diffusion research developed include sociology, anthropology, education, communication, and marketing.[8] The important

---

[5] Everett M. Rogers, 31-35.

[6] Ibid., 107-109.

[7] Everett M Rogers, and F. Floyd Shoemaker, *Communication of Innovations: A Cross-Cultural Approach* (New York, NY: The Free Press, 1971), 45.

[8] Rogers and Shoemaker, 45-76.

point to glean from this is that diffusion of innovations is extremely important and widely accepted across many academic disciplines. Of these, this work will focus on anthropology, sociology, and communication theory because these disciplines contribute most to the required analysis of USG efforts in Afghanistan.

Because the theory evolved in each tradition independently from the other traditions, there are some key differences in the conceptualization of the theory between disciplines. Anthropological studies tend to focus on how modern Western ideas diffuse across primitive societies. Therefore, the anthropological tradition aligns with Lawrence Brown, Professor of Geography, who focuses on the exchange of ideas between societies and how those exchanges generate social change.[9] In this regard, the anthropological tradition is very helpful in the analysis of USG efforts in Afghanistan. However, this study is also concerned with how those innovations spread throughout the society once introduced.

Early sociological research conducted by scholars like Gabriel Tarde tended to focus on the effects of diffusion of innovations on social change. Rural sociology claims the largest and most enduring tradition of diffusion research. Ryan and Gross' research in 1943 on the diffusion of hybrid corn seed in rural Iowa is a seminal work in this tradition because it led to deeper research into the roles of various communication channels and their effect on the innovation-decision process.[10] This tradition also provides important insights into USG efforts in Afghanistan because the communication channel employed to disseminate information about USG programs can be critical in the rate of their adoption.

Finally, the communication discipline has demonstrated a strong tradition in diffusion research. Rogers and his colleague, Floyd Shoemaker, highlight that since the 1960s communication researchers have focused on the transmission of technological ideas in less developed nations. Therefore, the communication tradition of diffusion research may be the most important to the discussion of USG efforts

---

[9] Ibid., 49.

[10] Ibid., 53-54.

in Afghanistan. The strength of the communication tradition is that it can analyze any type of innovation. This enables the communication researcher to focus on the process of diffusion.[11]

With the evolution of diffusion research explained, next it is important to understand and define the theory. Rogers defines diffusion as "the process by which an innovation is communicated through certain channels over time among the members of a social system."[12] He defines innovation as "an idea, practice or object perceived as new to an individual or other unit of adoption."[13] Clearly, people most often equate innovation to technology or the hardware of a new idea; the cell phone or computer for example. However, Rogers emphasizes that an idea, like a political philosophy or a religion, can be an innovation.[14] He identifies diffusion of innovations as a special form of communication because the messages relate to new ideas. This is particularly important because new ideas come with a level of uncertainty for the individual. This uncertainty slows the adoption of innovations because of the perceptions of a lack of predictability and a lack of understanding of the advantages of the new idea over others.[15]

Lawrence Brown, a geography professor at Ohio State, defines diffusion slightly differently. In his 1981 book, *Innovation Diffusion: A New perspective*, He states diffusion is; "the process by which innovation spreads from one locale or one social group to another."[16] Additionally, Michael Webber in a review of Brown's book highlights one of Brown's observations, which is critical to the application of diffusion of innovations in the Afghanistan scenario. Webber states, "he [Brown] recognized, first, that the suppliers of innovations have a role to play in encouraging their adoption– by adapting the innovation to people's tastes and pockets; by establishing agencies through which the innovation is distributed to the

---

[11] Rogers and Shoemaker, 66-67.

[12] Ibid., 5.

[13] Rogers, 12.

[14] Ibid., 13.

[15] Ibid.

[16] Lawrence A. Brown, *Innovation Diffusion: A New Perspective* (New York, NY: Methuen & Co., 1981), 1.

population; and by encouraging its use."[17] Webber notes that the essence of Brown's insight was in the observation that diffusion of innovations reflects supplier behavior as well as adopter behavior.[18]

At first glance, Rogers' and Brown's definitions may seem to only differ in minor semantics. However, when examined more closely the definitions are significantly different and both taken together contribute to a more nuanced understanding of diffusion of innovations. Rogers' definition focuses on the diffusion of ideas within a social system while Brown's definition clearly emphasizes the diffusion of an innovation from one social system to another. Undoubtedly, evidence abounds to suggest that both are occurring. Therefore, a new hybrid definition of diffusion of innovations is necessary. This new definition encompasses both phenomenon and better serves to examine and explain the diffusion of governance and development innovations in Afghanistan. Therefore, diffusion of innovations is defined as the process by which an innovation is communicated from one social system to another and subsequently how that innovation spreads through the new social system.

While Brown's definition is slightly different from Rogers and focuses on the diffusion of ideas from one social system to another, this does not mean that Rogers' concepts about diffusion of innovations do not apply to diffusion of this type. Rogers clearly highlights in his works numerous instances where his diffusion concepts apply to the study diffusion from one culture to another. For instance in *Diffusion of Innovations* Rogers highlights a research project conducted by scholars Paul Deutschmann and Orlando Fals Borda who introduced new farm innovations in a Columbian village in the 1960s. This study demonstrated Rogers' concept of an "S" shaped diffusion curve and categories of adopters. [19] Another project Rogers cites, as an example of his concept of sustainability, is the efforts of Dr "Chicken" Davis, a U.S. poultry science expert, to introduce American chickens to Nigeria in an

---

[17] Michael Webber, "Classics in Human Geography Revisited: Brown, L. A. Innovation Diffusion: A New Perspective. London: Methuen, Commentary 1." *Progess in Human Geography*, (2006): 487.

[18] Ibid., 488.

[19] Rogers, 268.

attempt to provide greater nutrition to the Nigerian people.[20] These two examples demonstrate that, while Rogers did not specifically mention diffusion from one social system to another in his definition, he clearly believes it is an integral part of diffusion research and his characteristics apply to this kind of diffusion as well.

With diffusion of innovations fully defined, next it is important to understand the major elements of the concept. Rogers identifies four main elements of diffusion of innovations. These elements are the social system in which the diffusion takes place, the communication channel, the innovation itself, and time.[21] These elements are important because are the key variables, which affect the rate of adoption of the innovation. In most applications of the diffusion model, organizations want to isolate and decrease the time variable. Time is the variable most organizations want to affect and therefore, addressed first.

If an organization or business is trying to promote a certain idea, they want it to diffuse across the target audience as quickly as possible. Therefore, time is the variable the organization tries to decrease through the manipulation of aspects of the other three. Likewise, in an analysis of governance and development efforts in Afghanistan, the key desire is for the Afghan people to adopt USG programs as quickly as possible. Rogers states this case well in the introduction of his book when he writes:

> Getting a new idea adopted, even when it has obvious advantages, is difficult. Many innovations require a lengthy period of many years from the time when they become available to the time when they are widely adopted. Therefore, a common problem for many individuals and organizations is how to speed up the rate of diffusion of an innovation.[22]

Some organizations attempt to manipulate the perceived characteristics of an innovation in an effort to speed up its rate of adoption. Diffusion scholars have long examined how the perceived characteristics of the innovation itself affect the rate of adoption. To aid in this analysis, Rogers identifies five perceived attributes; *relative advantage, compatibility, complexity, trialability and observability.*

---

[20] Rogers, 376.

[21] Ibid., 11.

[22] Ibid., 1.

Relative advantage is the degree to which potential adopters perceive an innovation as better than the idea it supersedes. The greater degree potential adopters perceive innovations as advantageous in a social system, the quicker it will diffuse. Rogers defines *compatibility* as the degree to which potential adopters perceive an innovation is consistent with existing values, past experiences and needs.[23] In other words, the degree to which an innovation is compatible with the culture or the social system is a critical determinant in its rate of diffusion. *Complexity* deals with the potential adopter's perceptions about how difficult the innovation is to understand and use. The more complex a person perceives an innovation to be, the slower it will diffuse. *Trialability* deals with the ability of potential adopters to test the innovation without converting completely. If potential adopters can try the innovation before making a complete transition, they are more likely to adopt the innovation and it will diffuse more quickly across the social system. Finally, Rogers defines *observability* as the degree to which the results of an innovation are visible to others.[24] Obviously, for the innovation to diffuse successfully, a potential adopter must perceive those observations as advantageous.

The attributes of an innovation are useful as an analytical tool. An individual or organization wishing to diffuse an innovation can analyze the innovation's attributes with relation to the social system in order to determine its efficacy to individuals in the system. If certain aspects of the innovation do not seem to meet the positive criteria of the perceived attributes, the organization can tailor its messages to the target audience. For example, the organization can utilize messages that highlight the advantages of the innovation or make the innovation seem more compatible to the social system. The organization could present information to individuals demonstrating the use of the innovation hence reducing its complexity. Perhaps the organization can determine a way to make the innovation "tryable" for the target social system. Finally, determining a way to make the innovation and its advantages observable to as many people as possible across the social system can greatly help the diffusion process.

---

[23] Rogers, 15.

[24] Ibid., 16.

8

However, communicative processes concerning the innovation greatly affect the perceptions of the innovation's advantages. Therefore, the potential adopter's perceptions about the innovation are closely linked to the communication process. Brown emphasizes this point when he states, "the adoption of an innovation is primarily the outcome of a learning or communication process. Accordingly, a fundamental step in examining the process of diffusion is identification of factors related to the effective flow of information and of the characteristics of information flows, information reception, and resistances to adoption."[25] In other words, if an individual or organization, wishing to diffuse an innovation understands how the people in the social system will perceive the innovation, they can tailor the communication messages and channels to maximize the diffusion effect.

This leads to the second main element of diffusion of innovations, which is the communication channel. The channel is critical because it can determine the number of people a message reaches, how quickly it reaches them and if the message is influential. Everett Rogers states that usually mass media is the quickest and most efficient way of informing the largest possible audience about an innovation.[26] However, the infrastructure of the country and the culture has a great deal of influence on the effectiveness of the communication channel. If the population does not trust a mass media channel or the channel does not reach large portions of the population due to a lack of infrastructure or an austere environment, it will be less effective or worse, ineffective.

A critical lesson learned through diffusion research is that most people depend on another similar person's subjective evaluation of an innovation.[27] In other words, when an individual receives positive information about an innovation from a person who is similar to them and has already tried the innovation, the individual is more likely to adopt the innovation. Therefore, the more similar the adopter is to the person with whom he is communicating about an innovation, the more likely the other person

---

[25] Brown, 6.

[26] Rogers, 18.

[27] Ibid., 18-19.

will adopt the innovation. Scholars in psychology have found that similarity is a powerful influencing mechanism. Robert Cialdini notes that in several research studies sameness was a significant variable in persuading people to do something.[28] This phenomenon reveals an important potential problem in the diffusion of an innovation. Usually, the individuals trying to diffuse an innovation are very different from the people they are trying to persuade to adopt it. This is what Rogers calls *heterophily*.[29] This is obviously the case with USG officials in Afghanistan. Therefore, the challenge is figuring out how to diffuse an innovation through a communication channel that is similar to the target audience of potential adopters. Rogers recommends the use of opinion leaders. Rogers defines opinion leaders as members of the target audiences' social system who are "able to influence other individual's attitudes or overt behavior informally in a desired way with relative frequency."[30]

The fourth element of diffusion is the social system. Rogers defines a social system as "a set of interrelated units (individuals) that are engaged in joint problem solving to accomplish a common goal."[31] For the purposes of this study, the social system is Afghanistan as a whole. While many sub cultures exist in the tribal and clan composition of the Afghan nation and culture, it is well beyond the scope of this work to delve into every aspect of these sub cultures and how they interact. A work of such magnitude would take several volumes and years of dedicated research. However, the social system is critically important. It affects perceptions and attitudes about innovations and therefore can be a strong determining factor in rates of adoption.

---

[28] Robert Cialdini, *Influence: Science and Practice* (Needham Heights, MA: Allyn and Bacon, 2001) 150-151. Cialdini cites one study conducted by Evans in 1963 where people were more likely to buy insurance from an agent who was similar in age, religion, politics and smoking habits. Cialdini also notes that the influence of similarity is so strong that many sales training programs urge trainees to "mirror and match" body posture, mood and verbal style of customers.

[29] Rogers, 19.

[30] Ibid., 27.

[31] Ibid., 23.

The Afghan Social System

While it is well beyond the scope of the work to delve into every nuance of Afghan and Islamic culture, a basic understanding of the complex social system in which the USG operates is essential to understanding why Afghans fail to adopt USG initiatives. As Westerners, we can only hope to have a basic understanding of the Afghan culture. The nuances and latent features of the culture are too complex for an outsider to understand fully. Afghan culture is a unique mix of ethnic, tribal and religious variables.

The first, and perhaps most important, characteristic of Afghan culture is the strong tie Afghans have to their family, tribe and clan. These relationships typically form the strongest bonds in Afghan culture and are stronger than the concepts of nation or province. There are a vast number of ethnic groups resident in the country. This means the population's allegiances vary from region to region and tribe to tribe. Few Afghans automatically feel any allegiance to a larger national government or concept of nation unless the national power is from their ethnic group or tribe. This is evident in the way Afghans vote in elections. In a recent report to Congress, Kenneth Katzman illustrates this point when he states, "in spite of Afghanistan's post-Taliban political and economic modernization, patterns of political affiliation along family, clan, tribe, ethnicity, and region remain."[32] Additionally, he notes that these patterns are even more evident in provincial elections.[33]

Many ethnic groups have their own languages and dialects further hampering national unity and many ethnic groups are sub-divided into several tribes. It is difficult to put an exact number on the ethnic and tribal permutations that exist in Afghanistan. Two books *Afghanistan, a Country Study* and *Culture and Customs of Afghanistan* identify at least 18 different ethnic groups, numerous tribes aligned under each ethnic group (depending on the group) and at least forty-nine different languages and dialects.[34]

---

[32] Kenneth Katzman, *Afghanistan: Politics, Elections, and Government Performance* (Congressional Report, Washington DC: Congressional Research Service, 2011) 2.

[33] Ibid.

[34] Hafizullah Emadi, *Culture and Customs of Afghanistan* (Westport, CT: Greenwood Press, 2005) 7-12.

Adding another layer of confusion to this already complex cultural stew are the different sects of Islam, which include Sunni, Shia, Ismailis and Sufis. To a certain extent, these sects align with particular ethnic groups and tribes (See Table 1).[35] Other religious groups are present, including Sikhs, Hindus and Christians, but they exert little to no influence in the country.[36]

The predominant ethnic group in Afghanistan is Pashtu. This means the Pashtu sub-culture has an enormous influence on the country as a whole. Anthropologist, Jon Anderson states, "Pashtuns have historically dominated government, other ethnic groups have had to learn to deal with them on the Pashtun's own terms." This "Pashtunization" of the culture has led to the strong influence of the Pashtunwali code on the culture. The Pashtunwali code includes honor and the defense of honor, autonomy, bravery, self-respect, and respect for others.[37]

The complex and nuanced cocktail of ethnic, tribal, regional, and religious influences creates an Afghan culture rife with divisiveness as groups struggle to gain power and control. Therefore, any similarities amongst the different groups are largely ignored and insignificant and a united Afghan nation remains elusive. Pashtuns in governmental positions tend to side with other Pashtuns regardless of the circumstances.[38] Similar circumstances occur wherever one tribe enjoys the majority of power. Throughout Afghanistan's history, this has tended to lead to internal strife, warlordism and civil war. The editors of *Afghanistan: a Country Study* state, "scholars studying Afghanistan quip that if Afghans were not fighting soldiers of another country, they would be fighting one another."[39] This illustrates the challenges the USG faces as it tries to enable, support and expand a strong central and democratic form of government in Afghanistan.

---

[35] Emadi, 7-12.

[36] Ibid., 21.

[37] Nyrop and Seekins, 108.

[38] Ibid., 112.

[39] Ibid.

Another factor affecting governance rests with the elites of the country. Like many other countries a multi-tiered social stratum is prevalent in Afghanistan with powerful elites residing at the top. An important distinction exists between urban and rural elite. Urban elites hold most of the powers in the central government and, as stated earlier, predominantly arise from the Pashtu ethnic group. However, the rural elites exert enormous amounts of influence at the local level. This is due to several factors. First, Hafizullah Emadi notes the rural elites have a grassroots understanding of politics in their communities and can exert influence over an immense number of people. Other factors include the difficult terrain, ethnic and tribal influences, and lack of infrastructure limiting the influence of the central government in

_____

remote areas. Emadi states that relationships develop between urban and rural elite based on mutual benefit and cooperation.[41] Clerics and tribal chiefs represent another group of significant influencers in Afghan politics. Clerics and tribal chiefs can rally peasants to support political agendas and build influence through their ethnic, tribal or religious linkages. USG governance efforts must incorporate these key influencers in order to obtain maximum support from the Afghan population. USG planners can use their understanding of the symbiotic relationship between urban elites (central government officials) and rural elites to tailor governance initiatives to exert influence over the maximum area of the country and gain greater legitimacy for Afghan Government efforts. Elites, clerics and tribal chiefs are the opinion leaders in Afghan society.[42]

While Islam plays a significant role in Afghan life, it is less influential than ethnic and tribal factors. However, it still permeates Afghan culture from customs and traditions, to law and governance and therefore, in order to understand Afghan culture, one must understand Islam's influences on Afghanistan. First, Majid Khadduri states that Muslim thinkers believe that "the individual's rights and obligations were always defined in terms of (though subordinate to) the community's interests."[43] This means that Afghans care about their own self-interests, but try not to put them first. Afghans believe in the collective good. However, this does not mean Afghans blindly support the central or provincial government. When Afghans think of their Islamic duty to the group, they perceive that it pertains to their family, tribe or clan, not Afghanistan as a whole. For example, in his study of the Ghilzai tribe anthropologist, Jon Anderson, notes that Afghan Islam consists of three components – qawm (tribe), tariqa, and sharia. Anderson sees tribe as chief among these as the Ghilzai perceive their sense of umma as coming from the tribe itself therefore Afghans generally see tribal membership on par with

---

[41] Emadi, 21.

[42] Rogers, 388.

[43] Majid Khadduri, *War and Peace in the Law of Islam* (Baltimore, MD: Johns Hopkins University Press) 3.

membership in the Muslim community.[44] In this way, even in the context of Islam itself, tribe exerts a strong influence. Therefore, while Islam is an important contributor to Afghan culture and customs, tribe and ethnic group remain the most important.

Some scholars have argued that Afghanistan is plagued by a culture of corruption. It is no secret that corruption is rampant across the country. It is important to understand how corruption became so prevalent in the society. Several key factors contribute to Afghanistan's corruption problems. In his book, *Modern Afghanistan*, Amin Saikal argues that three factors led to Afghanistan's current plight. First, polygamy led to rivalries and struggles for power among offspring, which created instability and disunity within the country.[45] Secondly, foreign interference further weakened already feeble domestic structures. The foreign intervention and the rivalries created by polygamy caused competing factions within the country to vie for the resources (money, business, development, etc.) that the great powers brought to the country. Saikal contends that these destabilizing factors brought about the power vacuum, which allowed ideological extremism to flourish in Afghanistan.[46] It also set the conditions for a culture of corruption to take root. Afghans have grown up with war, rivalry and foreign intervention. The 2009 statistic for life expectancy in Afghanistan was 46 years.[47] This means that few Afghans can recall a period of relative peace and void of oppressive regimes. Afghans have grown up in an environment where survival means competing for power or buying off power. This environment has fostered corruption that permeates the society today. Exacerbating the issue is the billions of dollars the USG and other ISAF nations pump into the country for development. This complex dynamic means that USG officials must be very careful how they allocate funds and award development projects. Money and projects awarded to a member of one tribe or ethnic group can empower them at the risk of marginalizing other groups. Foreign money can

---

[44] Nyrop and Seekins, 99-100.

[45] Amin Saikal, *Modern Afghanistan: A History of Struggle and Survival.* (London: I. B. Tauris & Company Ltd., 2004), 4-6.

[46] Ibid., 3.

[47] United Nations, *"UNICEF,"* http://www.unicef.org/infobycountry/afghanistan_statistics.html \ (accessed January 10, 2011).

upset an already tedious balance of power in volatile regions and in such a convoluted system; the money can easily find its way into insurgent hands.

Afghan history is also useful in understanding Afghan culture. An historical examination shows that Afghans have almost no Western democratic traditions. Katzman states, "At the national level Afghanistan had few, if any Western style democratic institutions prior to the international intervention that took place after September 11, 2001."[48] Additionally, he notes, "Afghanistan's governing structure has historically consisted of a weak central government."[49] He goes on to say that the tribal, clan and family structure, which characterized government at the local level and probably displayed the best hope for democratic principles was largely broken up by decades of war and Taliban rule as many traditional authority figures fled or were killed. The local power brokers who remained are less popular with the people and as the people perceive them selectively applying the law and only looking out for themselves. Some may argue that prior to Taliban rule; Afghanistan had a democratic government in the form of a constitutional monarchy. However, Katzman notes that during this time, the parliament was never a significant check on King Zahir Shah's powers.[50]

In April 1978 Peoples Democratic Party of Afghanistan (PDPA), a communist political party came to power as a result of the Saur (April) Rebellion. Their two presidents, Taraki and Amin, attempted to institute radical social change by redistributing land and placing women in governmental positions. The Afghans, especially the members of the Islamic parties, rebelled to these initiatives. This was a significant contributing factor to the Soviet invasion and the rise of the *Mujahedin.*[51]

These few historical examples demonstrate significant obstacles for the USG as it attempts to promote good democratic governance in Afghanistan. First, the Afghan culture has few if any democratic

---

[48] Kenneth Katzman, *Afghanistan: Politics, Elections, and Government Performance* (Congressional Report, Washington DC: Congressional Research Service, 2011), 1.

[49] Ibid.

[50] Ibid.

[51] Katzman, Kenneth. *Afghanistan:Current Issues and U.S. Policy Concerns.* Congressional Report, (Washington DC: Congressional Research Service, Library of Congress, 2001), 1.

traditions. Secondly, the central government has never been able to exert much influence over the 80 percent of the rural population.[52] Finally, generally, the population is opposed to very radical liberal changes, and is rife with the ingredients that promote corruption.

A key asset in helping USG officials understand the social system is the Human Terrain Team (HTT). The USG first employed HTTs in February 2007 in Eastern Afghanistan. HTTs are groups of civilian anthropologists and social scientists who advise combat units about cultural issues, tribal customs and beliefs. The great advantage provided by HTTs rests in their ability to provide immediate nuanced cultural understanding that combat commanders could only hope to gain after years of operating in Afghanistan (or other locations). For example, in one instance an HTT anthropologist who witnessed the Taliban behead a tribal elder recognized their goals were more than mere intimidation. The anthropologist advised the combat commander that the Taliban was attempting to divide and weaken the Zadran tribe, one of Southeastern Afghanistan's most powerful, in an attempt to gain power in the area. The anthropologist advised that if the U.S. forces could preserve and strengthen the Zadran tribe, they could block the Talban from the area. With this information, the commander dispersed units into remote areas to conduct Shuras to resolve tribal differences.[53] In this and countless other instances, the HTTs have proven their worth as a combat multiplier on the battlefield.

HTTs demonstrate that the USG realizes the importance of the social system and its effect on the Afghan people's adoption of governance and development innovations it is trying to diffuse across Afghanistan. HTTs are a promising step in the right direction and address one of Rogers' key components of diffusion of innovations.

Afghan Communication Channels

How information concerning an innovation flows across the social system can greatly affect its rate of adoption. Sometimes the difference between adoption and rejection of an innovation is simply the

---

[52] Katzman, *Afghanistan: Politics Elections and Government Performance*, 2.

[53] Anonymous. "Social Science Teams Aid Army in Afghanistan," *Army Magazine*, December, 2007, 73.

communication channel through which information about the innovation flows. Therefore understanding the Afghan's preferred communication channels is very important. Understanding which channels (mediums) Afghans prefer to communicate through allows USG officials to tailor messages to reach the largest possible number of potential adopters.

The most important communication channel (medium) in Afghanistan is radio. Radio is the most accessible media for Afghan households with eighty-two percent of respondents to the *Afghanistan Survey 2010* saying they own a functioning radio. There is little difference in radio ownership between urban and rural areas.[54]

However, while radio may reach the most people, the most persuasive form of communication is word of mouth. Word of mouth, therefore, is the second most critical communication channel (medium). Around one in five respondents (nineteen percent) to the *Afghanistan Survey 2010* depend on friends and family to receive news and information.[55] The survey goes on to say,

> The use of oral communication to get news and information is high, with more than half of respondents using meetings in the community and sermons in mosques for this purpose, showing that traditional means of information dissemination continue to remain important in Afghan society. Respondents continue to prefer to get information on local news and events from personal acquaintances rather than leadership figures within their community.[56]

While radio reaches the most people and therefore is the best quantitative medium, word of mouth is the most effective means of persuasion or the best qualitative medium. Therefore, any comprehensive information campaign in Afghanistan must saturate both these communication channels. The challenge to USG officials with regard to the latter, word of mouth communication is that in order for it to be effective, it must originate from a personal acquaintance.

---

[54] Mohammad Osman Tariq, Najla Ayoubi, Fazel Habi Haqbeen, *Afghanistan in 2010: A Survey of the Afghan People.* (Kabul, Afghnistan: The Asia Foundation, 2010), 7.

[55] Ibid.

[56] Ibid., 37.

In his discussion of change agents, Rogers talks about the problem of perceived *heterophily* (difference) between the target population and the change agent. He suggests that change agents can accelerate the diffusion process by employing opinion leaders within the social system to advocate the innovations.[57] The change agent in this case is the USG. The USG does not have much, if any, *homophily* (similarity) with the target population. Rogers identifies this as a substantial obstacle to adoption. Therefore, enlisting opinion leaders in the Afghan community can greatly improve the chances of Afghans adopting and using development and governance initiatives. As stated earlier in the section on Afghan culture, some of these important opinion leaders would include religious imams and tribal elders. Enlisting these kinds of people to champion USG development and governance initiatives can put an Afghan face on the programs and increase the likelihood of Afghans adopting these innovations.

Development Initiatives

Some of the most important development initiatives currently underway in Afghanistan are in the Agricultural sector of its economy. Almost 80 percent of the population is, in some way, linked to agriculture.[58] Forty-seven percent of people in Afghanistan identify their occupation as either farmer or farm laborer.[59] Obviously the USG promotes many other development projects in Afghanistan. These include construction of bridges, roads, irrigation, health clinics and schools. The USG infuses billions of dollars into these projects. For instance, USAID contributed more than $11.5 million in development assistance programs since 2002.[60] Also since 2002, the U.S. Military has appropriated $62 billion for relief and reconstruction efforts with $2.64 billion for the Commander's Emergency Response Program

---

[57] Rogers, 27, 388.

[58] Rondal L. Turner, "Agricultural Development Teams and the Counterinsurgency in Afghanistan." (Research Project, US Army War College, Carlisle, PA, US Army War College, 2010), 1.

[59] Tariq et al., 158.

[60] Charles M Johnson Jr., "USAID Continues to Face Challenges in Managing and Overseeing U.S. Development Assistance Programs," Congressional Testimony, http://www.gao.gov/products/GA-10-932T (accessed December 28, 2011).

(CERP).[61] This work focuses on agricultural initiatives for several reasons. First, unlike infrastructure projects, agricultural initiatives offer Afghan farmers a choice to adopt. Most people do not make a conscious choice about whether they use a road or bridge. If it is there, and helps them, they will use it without much thought. Second, agricultural development initiatives are critical programs in Afghanistan where almost half (47 percent) of the population work in the agricultural industry.[62] Finally, there is sufficient literature and data concerning agricultural development initiatives to adequately analyze these programs utilizing diffusion of innovations theory. In spite of the limitations to analysis, evidence suggests that other development programs face the same challenges of agricultural initiatives. Ms. Lorraine Sherman, a representative for the U.S. Agency for International Development (USAID) notes, many Afghans are not using or maintaining many of these projects.[63]

Much of the arable land in Afghanistan goes unused primarily due to Afghan farmers' lack of knowledge of modern farming techniques.[64] Therefore, the goal of many USG sponsored and funded agricultural development programs is to teach the Afghan population better farming techniques which will lead to bigger crop yields and subsequent economic growth. An integral part of the implementation of these programs at the operational level is the Agricultural Development Team (ADT). ADTs in Afghanistan are usually assigned at the provincial level. However because these elements are limited, not every province gets an ADT. Some of the initiatives ADTs introduce include classroom instruction on

---

[61] Gregory Johnson, Vijaya Ramachandran, and Julie Walz, "The Commander's Emergency Response Program in Afghanistan: Five Practical Recommendations." *Center for Global Development,* http://www.cgdev.org/files/1425413_file_Johnson_Ramachandran_Walz_CERP_brief.pdf (accessed December 28, 2011).

[62] Tariq et al., 219. In the Afghanistan Survey 2010, thirty-four percent of respondents identified their occupation as "farmer" while another thirteen percent identified as "farm laborer." These figures do not account for the many other jobs and industries that support agriculture or rely on agriculture to support their industries. When these are considered, it can be assumed that well over half the population significantly relies on agriculture for their livelihood.

[63] Sherman, 5.

[64] Turner, 1.

better farming practices during non-growing seasons, animal husbandry, bee keeping, and livestock production.[65]

By far the greatest obstacle the ADTs face is the illegal cultivation of opium poppy. This presents a significant problem for both the Afghan Government and coalition forces.[66] Additionally, as former Chairman of the Joint Chiefs of Staff, Admiral Mullen, has noted the poppy trade fuels the insurgency as insurgents purchase, funnel and sell poppy for profit[67]. Poppy farmers do not necessarily ally with insurgents for ideological reasons, but primarily for economic reasons. The widespread and virtually unimpeded growth of poppy delegitimizes the Afghan government since poppy cultivation is illegal. Therefore, a major goal of the ADTs is to introduce legal commercial crops to replace the opium poppy. This represents a shift from the previous hard-line approach taken in the middle of the decade when the Afghan Government implemented widespread eradication measures. These tactics risked pushing poppy farmers' loyalties towards the insurgents. Therefore, in recent years, efforts to introduce alternative crops have emerged as a possible viable alternative and the ADT is a key element in the implementation of these efforts. Some of the potential substitute crops include wheat, grapes, pomegranates, almonds, and dates.[68]

Analysis of Development Initiatives

Afghans are not adopting the development programs the USG is promoting because these programs fail to conform to the primary elements of diffusion of innovations, including the communication channel and perceived attributes of an innovation. Among the three reasons Ms. Sherman cites for why Afghans are indifferent about USG development projects, is that some Afghans apparently

---

[65] Turner 11.

[66] Ibid., 2.

[67] Michael J. Carden, "Narcotics Trade Fuels Afghanistan Insurgency, Mullen Says." *American Forces Press Service*, Sepetember 19, 2008.

[68] Turner, 3.

harbor ill feelings towards the United States or some Afghans align with the Taliban.[69] This illustrates the USG's lack of consideration for the communication channel as officials work to diffuse development programs throughout Afghanistan. If U.S. officials want Afghans to use these projects, but some Afghans harbor ill feelings towards the United States, it is imperative that the projects have an Afghan face. Someone from the community must champion these projects. This is where the USG must solicit the help of tribal leaders and imams. Putting an Afghan face on these projects could overcome the first problem Ms. Sherman mentions. In addition, tribal leaders and imams immersed in the culture will be better able to tailor the communication messages about the innovations to the Afghan people they are trying to persuade.

Another contributing factor to the slow adoption of development programs is their failure to adequately demonstrate positive attributes of innovation. First among these attributes is the perception of *relative advantage*. Virtually all aspects, the alternative crop initiatives fail to meet the first test of perceived attributes of innovation *relative advantage*. Take the Pomegranate as an example. Pomegranate trees can produce fruit after a year but usually it takes two and a half to three years to produce fruit. In contrast, poppy produces in the same year of sowing.[70] Another factor is the Afghan market. Martin Wuisthuis explains how the Afghan market affects the decision to grow poppy instead of pomegranates. He states, "in the imperfect Afghan market system, the farmer does not know what the price will do tomorrow or next week, nor does he have the storage facilities to abide his time. The drug traffickers show up with advanced payment, credit, contract farming and technical advice." Wuisthuis further notes "[it is a] whole package which is difficult to resist when your family is starving."[71] Pomegranate diffusion

---

[69] Sherman, 5.

[70] Weusthuis, Martin, *Afghan Pomegranates in the Netherlands: Designing an International Pomegranate Supply Chain,* Thesis (Van Hall Larstein Universtiy of Applied Sciences, Wageningen, The Netherlands: Van Hall Larstein Universtiy of Applied Sciences, 2009), 25.

[71] Ibid.

fails because it takes multiple growing seasons to reap a crop and pomegranates do not command as much profit therefore demonstrating little or no *relative advantage* to the Afghan farmer.

Wheat does not fare any better although it is the main seasonal competitor to poppy.[72] The primary reason for this is simply price. In 2010, a hectare of wheat might fetch $440 at market while the same area of land cultivated with poppy earned a farmer five times as much.[73] Afghan farmers interviewed in a recent Frontline program titled "Opium Brides" cite this fact repeatedly. In fact, many farmers feel they have no other choice.[74] Wheat can be harvested in the same season, but as stated above, is five times less profitable than poppy. Until the USG and ADTs find a crop that is as easy to cultivate and harvest as poppy and can command a similar price on the market, Afghans will probably not adopt alternative crops because they see no *relative advantage* over the cultivation of poppy.

Some may argue that the Afghan Government's poppy eradication policy has the effect of giving alternative crops a *relative advantage* because the government will not destroy the alternative crops. However, this is only effective in areas near cities where the government can exert significant control. In the Frontline presentation, one Afghan farmer stated that if he were further from the city where the government could not exert control he would grow poppy. Therefore, wherever the government can exert control and the threat of poppy eradication is high, some farmers may adopt alternative crops. However, as stated earlier, this threat has the adverse effect of pushing populations towards support to the Taliban and the insurgency. In this way, an effort in the development line of effort can negatively affect efforts in the governance line of effort. Compounding this problem, instances of violence have occurred when the Afghan Police attempt to eradicate poppy crops. In one instance, Afghan Police fired on farmers who rioted and demonstrated against the poppy eradication measures.[75] In places where the government cannot

---

[72] Turner, 4.

[73] Ibid.

[74] *Frontline,* "Opium Bride," PBS, January 3, 2012.

[75] Ibid.

exert its influence, it loses legitimacy from the outset because it has created a law it cannot completely enforce.

USG officials also failed to capitalize fully on the attribute of *compatibility* as highlighted by Ms. Sherman's third reason why Afghans do not use USG development projects. She states, "some Afghans support the U.S. effort and live in relatively friendly controlled districts, but they are not solicited for input into the design or implementation of the projects. Therefore, many Afghans perceive the projects as foreign".[76] If officials consulted with local Afghans during the design phase, the officials could have tailored the projects and messages about the projects to fit neatly into the Afghan culture. This would have ensured that the innovations were *compatible* with the Afghan culture (*social system*).

Perceptions of *compatibility* and *complexity* are closely related. Afghans may perceive some innovations as complex because the change agent (the USG) does not know how to communicate information about the program to the Afghan people. If the USG employs opinion leaders immersed in the culture to champion programs, there is the added benefit that these opinion leaders can devise ways to simplify the innovations and make them easier to use reducing their *complexity*. Making the innovations less complex to the Afghan people could encourage more adoption.

Another retardant to the Afghan's adoption of USG development initiatives is the fact that many programs do not offer much *trialability*. For instance, Ms. Sherman's second cited reason for Afghans not using USG projects and services is that some segments of the population do not support the Taliban, but the projects are in Taliban controlled regions and therefore the population is afraid to use or maintain the services.[77] If Afghans fear for their lives or the lives of their families if they adopt an innovation, adoption of that innovation will be severely limited. Therefore, the security situation has a profound effect on the perceived *trialability* of USG programs.

---

[76] Sherman, 5.

[77] Ibid.

Alternative crop programs do not offer much *trialability* to the Afghan farmer either. Additionally, it is hard for Afghan farmers to dedicate a portion of their fields to growing grapes, almonds and pomegranates, which may take several years to produce significant yields, and hence profits. Every acre that Afghan farmers dedicate to these alternative crops reduces his potential profits and money in his pocket.

Finally, *observability* is a difficult attribute to demonstrate to Afghan farmers. It takes at least a growing season, and in many cases several growing seasons for them to see the advantages of alternative crops. Afghan farmers have to take considerable risk when devoting a portion of their arable land to a new crop with no guarantees of comparable profits. Therefore, Afghan farmers do not adopt alternative crops quickly because it is hard for them to *observe* their advantages quickly.

Governance Initiatives

Governance is the USG's second critical line of effort. Some strategists believe that the quality and extent of Afghan Governance is the most crucial variable.[78] President Bush's initial policy shortly after the invasion of Afghanistan was "[to] try to rebuild [,] try to build a relatively strong central government and to assist Afghanistan's economy."[79] Additionally, U.S. leaders wished Afghanistan to develop a democratic form of government. The prevailing theory was that if a strong democratic government could take hold, it would deny violent extremists a safe haven to plan future attacks. This became a significant part of the "Bush Doctrine."[80] In a 2009 strategy review, the Obama Administration narrowed the official U.S. goals to "preventing terrorism safe haven in Afghanistan and Pakistan."[81]

---

[78] Kenneth Katzman,. *Afghanistan: Post Taliban Governenace, Security and U.S. Policy.* Report to Congress, (Washignton DC: Congressional Research Service, 2011), Summary.

[79] Ibid., 9.

[80] "The National Security Strategy of the United States." Washington DC: The White House, September 2002. Introduction letter by President George W. Bush. *Chronology: The Evolution of the Bush Doctrine.* Public Broadasting Service, http://www.pbs.org/wgbh/pages/frontline/shows/iraq/etc/cron.html (accessed February 28, 2012). The "Bush Doctrine," as it came to be known, evolved out of the September 11, 2001 attacks.

[81] Katzman, *Afghanistan: Post Taliban Governance, Security and U.S. Policy,* 9.

However, while the official policy may have narrowed in scope, little has changed in the approach on the ground and in some respects, the "nation building" efforts have expanded.[82]

One of the primary tools the USG employs to build good governance in Afghanistan is the Provincial Reconstruction Team (PRT). While the PRT also executes tasks along the reconstruction and development line of effort, their primary mission is to promote good governance and foster legitimacy for the Afghan government. The PRT is a relatively new entity for the U.S. military. PRTs were born out of the Coalition Humanitarian Liaison Cells that the U.S. military established in *Operation Enduring Freedom* in early 2002.[83] Since then, the Army inculcated the organization into doctrine in FM 3-07, *Stability Operations*. This manual, for the first time in codified doctrine, details the PRTs organization, its duties and responsibilities, and employment on the battlefield. The PRT is truly an interagency initiative. A typical PRT contains: six Department of State personnel; three senior military officers and staff; twenty Army civil affairs advisors; one Department of Agriculture representative; one Department of Justice representative; three international contractors; two USAID representatives; and a military or contract security force[84]

The Provincial Reconstruction Development Committee (PRDC) is an important tool PRTs use to determine and prioritize projects in the province. The PRDC contains a USAID representative, a civil affairs advisor, one or more PRT members, and host-nation officials. FM 3-07 states, "the combined military and civil efforts are required to reduce conflict while developing the local institutions to take the lead in national governance, the provision of basic services, fostering economic development, and

---

[82] Ibid.

[83] Robert M. Perito, "The U.S. Experience with Provincial Reconstruction Teams in Afghanistan: Lessons Identified" Special Report 2005, United States Institute of Peace Washignton, DC, http://www.usip.org/files/resources/sr152.pdf (accessed January 28, 2012)

[84] Department of the Army, Field Manual (FM) 3-07, *Stability and Support Operations,* October, 2008, (Washington, DC: Government Printing Office, 2008), F-3.

enforcement of rule of law."[85] A PRDC develops a list of potential projects after consulting with the national ministries, provincial authorities, and local citizens.[86]

FM 3-07 Stability and Support Operations also defines USAID's nine principles of reconstruction. They include ownership, capacity building, sustainability, selectivity, assessment, results, partnership, flexibility, and accountability. These principles guide more than just the work of the interagency as the USG relies on NGOs, private companies and donors for funding and development projects. The principle of ownership emphasizes the participation of the host nation in the establishment and implementation of development priorities. Capacity building is concerned with the transfer of technical knowledge and skills to host nation officials. Sustainability aims to ensure that selected projects will have a lasting effect on the society. Selectivity focuses efforts on the needs of the population, the interests of the United States and the commitment of government officials. The principle of assessment requires project designers to research and understand the target community ensuring that projects conform to local cultural conditions. The principle of results requires project implementers to consider if the project will achieve the desired objectives and outcomes. Partnership calls for close collaboration between non-governmental organizations (NGOs), USAID, and host nation government officials because the USG relies on NGOs and private donors to fund many projects. Flexibility requires agencies to be adaptive, anticipate problems and seize opportunities. Lastly, accountability aims to build transparency in the system and prevent corruption. [87]

There are some promising indicators that this solid doctrinal foundation is generating progress along the governance line of effort. Surveys of the Afghan populace demonstrate that they readily accept a democratic form of government. This is somewhat surprising considering Afghanistan's historical lack of democratic institutions. According to the *Afghanistan Survey 2010*, "Afghan popular support for the

---

[85] FM 3-07, F-1.

[86] Ibid., F-3.

[87] Ibid., C-1 – C-8.

application of democratic principles of governance is high and there are high levels of agreement with the democratic principle of equal rights for all groups to participation and representation in government."[88]

Another indicator of Afghans' increased confidence in democratic institutions is the steady rise in their satisfaction with the performance of the national government. The *Afghanistan Survey 2010* cites the rise from 67 percent in 2008 to 71 percent in 2009 to 73 percent in the most recent survey. [89] The Afghan people's increasing confidence in the Afghan National Army (ANA) and Afghan National Police (ANP) is also an indicator of improvement. The ANA and ANP represent the most visible manifestations of the national government for the people. A significant majority of respondents think the ANA (86 percent) and the ANP (77 percent) "help improve security," and believe "the ANP is efficient at arresting those who have committed crimes so that they can be brought to justice" (70 percent).[90]

A willingness to participate in the democratic process is yet another indicator of the Afghan people's acceptance of democratic institutions. Here again, indicators are positive. In the *Afghanistan Survey 2010*, all respondents were asked how likely they were to vote in the coming parliamentary elections. Almost three quarters (74 percent) said that they were likely to vote.[91] More than half (54 percent) of respondents said they feel they can have a significant degree of influence over government decisions.[92] Clearly, perceptions of the 2009 presidential elections have affected the Afghan people's confidence and the willingness to participate in electoral processes. A slight majority of respondents say that the 2009 Presidential elections were free and fair.[93]

Recently, USG governance efforts have shifted to focus more on developing local governance primarily because of slow development of the central government, geographical challenges, and because

---

[88] Tariq et al., 12.

[89] Ibid.

[90] Ibid., 69.

[91] Ibid., 112.

[92] Ibid., 96.

[93] Ibid., 13.

of corruption in the central government.[94] For instance, a U.S. civilian representative for Southern Afghanistan, Henry Ensher, noted in January 2011 "local governance efforts – including the self-generated formation of village councils- are expanding in concert with the security provided by the U.S. troop surge."[95] Afghans give high marks to local government, giving the most positive assessment to the performance of Provincial Councils (78 percent approve), followed by district authorities (61 percent approve) and municipalities (53 percent approve).[96]

In spite of all these promising trends, corruption continues to retard the growth of democratic governance and reduces the Afghan people's trust and confidence in government institutions and officials. The *Afghanistan Survey 2010* identified cheating in the vote count, buying of votes, restrictions to women's electoral participation, including men voting on behalf of women, and husbands not letting their wives vote, and intimidation of voters or party activists as significant problems with the 2009 elections. Afghans report that between a third and a half of contacts with core government institutions involve some level of corruption.[97] Additionally, fifty-two percent of Afghans fear encounters with the ANP with nineteen percent responding they would have a lot of fear this is probably mainly due to corruption. More than half of the respondents who had contact with ANP officers in the last year report having encountered some level of corruption in the form of payment.[98] On one hand, as mentioned earlier, the Afghan people's perception of the ANP is high, but, on the other hand, they still see them as corrupt. Until corruption is not a significant issue, democracy in Afghanistan will continue to be a fleeting prospect. Unfortunately, the USG can do little to change this problem and may possibly be making it worse. The billions of dollars the USG provides to Afghanistan for development and governance may be priming the corruption pumps.

---

[94] Katzman, *Afghanistan: Post Taliban Governance, Security and U.S. Policy,* 12.

[95] Ibid.

[96] Tariq et al., 5.

[97] Ibid., 7.

[98] Ibid., 37.

The security situation is another key factor that greatly affects the development of a central democratic government. Perhaps the most troubling assessment from the *Afghanistan Survey 2010* is that levels of fear to participate are on the rise.[99] The essence of democratic governance rests in the participation of the people, both in their voting and running for office. Unfortunately, the security situation dissuades many Afghans from participating. In the *Afghanistan Survey 2010* only thirty-nine percent of respondents said they would have no fear participating in National elections and only twenty-eight percent said they would have no fear running for office.[100]

Analysis of Governance Initiatives

Unlike the development line of effort, efforts in governance show promise. While complete success still eludes the USG, the results of the *Afghanistan Survey 2010* show that the Afghan people are starting to embraced the principles of a central and democratic form of government. An application of the elements of diffusion of innovations (*communication channel* and the perceived attributes of an innovation; *relative advantage, compatibility, complexity, trialability* and *observability*) reveals many of the reasons that Afghans are starting to turn the corner in adopting USG governance initiatives.

First, the USG's governance efforts in Afghanistan consider the *communication channel* through which information about governance is transmitted. The key concept repeatedly emphasized throughout doctrine is the consultation with and communication through the host nation officials. The PRTs communicate information about the programs through the host nation officials which ensures more *homophily* between messenger and receiver. This too promotes greater adoption. The principle of *ownership* also relates to the *communication channel*. If *ownership* by government officials is sufficiently demonstrated, then Afghans are more likely to adopt those programs because the communication originated from a more similar source.

---

[99] Tariq et al., 37.

[100] Ibid.

USG Governance efforts also demonstrate the first perceived attribute of innovation, *relative advantage*. For instance, the principle of ownership encourages the consultation of the host nation officials when determining development projects and needs. This ensures that projects meet real needs in the population. As the government meets the critical needs of the people in the community, the Afghan people's confidence in their government will grow. As their confidence grows, they will perceive their new government as a *relative advantage* over the old system. When properly implemented, the principle of sustainability can demonstrate *relative advantage* as well. If projects demonstrate lasting improved effects to the people, these projects will be seen as a *relative advantage*. Finally, selectivity can also demonstrate a *relative advantage* as it concentrates efforts on infrastructure projects that focus, among other considerations, on ground-level needs and requirements.[101]

On the other hand, USG governance initiatives face challenges in demonstrating *compatibility* with the Afghan culture. The goal of instituting a strong central democratic form of government has little precedence in Afghanistan. As mentioned earlier, Afghans relate more to tribe and clan than to a central government in Kabul. Geography and corruption further hinder the establishment and effect of a strong central democratic government. The austere, rural environment, extreme topography and limited road networks severely limit the influence officials in Kabul can exert on the periphery. Corruption delegitimizes government institutions and pushes individual loyalties back to trusted entities like tribe and clan. The one bright spot in this area is the recent focal shift to local governance. This is a good development because it aligns nicely with the natural tendencies of Afghan culture – it is *compatible*.

The attribute of *complexity* is illustrated through the USAID principle of assessment as it requires agencies to assess local conditions, adapt best practices and design projects to fit local conditions.[102] This ensures that projects and information about them is tailored to the local people to make them easily implementable and understandable.

---

[101] FM 3-07, C-4.

[102] Ibid.

Trialability represents another challenge to USG governance efforts. The prevalence of corruption throughout the government limits the trust and confidence ordinary Afghans have in their government making it less likely that they will participate (*trialability*). The poor security situation deters many Afghans from participating in the government, both through voting in elections and running for office.[103] Finally, as long as the Afghan people perceive the ANP as corrupt and fear them the ability to test (*trialability*) the innovation of a strong democratic central government will be difficult.

Demonstrating the attribute of *observability* also remains a challenge. As mentioned earlier, the rural and tribal nature of Afghan culture and geography limit the central government's effect on common Afghans making it difficult to observe the new governmental system. This trend has not changed since ISAF arrived. Prior to 2009, the central government controlled a mere thirty percent of the country. Insurgents controlled approximately four percent. Tribes and local groups with varying degrees of loyalty to the central government controlled the remainder of the country; almost seventy percent.[104] The recent shift of focus to local governance is a promising development because it makes governance more *observable* to the ordinary Afghan.

The analysis presented above shows a mix of results. In many cases, Afghans have confidence in the democratic process and national government. However, the system continues to be plagued by corruption. The verdict remains out on whether Afghans will fully embrace a strong central democratic form of government. In the meantime, U.S. officials are taking many steps in the right direction.

Implications for the Operational Artist

Operational planners and Commanders can benefit from the analysis above and the application of diffusion research. This study demonstrates that in Afghanistan, and other operational theaters requiring full spectrum operations, diffusion research can be very helpful in the design of lines of effort. It can be particularly helpful in the governance, and development and reconstruction arenas. Additionally, diffusion

---

[103] Tariq et al., 8.

[104] Katzman, *Afghanistan: Post Taliban Governenace, Security and U.S. Policy,* 17.

of innovations can aid planners in determining the measures of effectiveness for programs within those lines of effort. For example, operational headquarters can measure rates of adoption of innovations (programs) across time. Operational commanders and planners can assess through data collection the local population's perceptions of innovation attributes like *relative advantage*, *trialability* and *complexity* to determine if programs are diffusing through the target population. Coalition efforts in Afghanistan already employ personnel to collect atmospherics to gauge the sentiments of the population. It would be easy to include collection tools targeting these desired measures into their mission set as soldiers circulate around the battlefield collecting atmospheric data.

The analysis above demonstrates that the *communication channel* through which information about a program flows is an important variable in its rate of adoption. Operational planners seeking a truly integrated and synchronized campaign plan should consult with Information Operations planners, Human Terrain Teams, ADT and PRT personnel to determine program goals, understand culture and media preferences and then tailor information messages and messengers to persuade the populace to adopt these programs. Planning must include ways to use opinion leaders within the populace who are most like the population to champion the innovations further increasing the potential for adoption.

Planners must understand the benefits of the innovations from the population's point of view, leverage these benefits and in some cases, when possible, adapt the innovation to accommodate greater benefits. Planners must not assume because they see the obvious advantages of an innovation that the target population will too. Rogers specifically cautions against this tendency. He calls it the pro innovation bias.[105] Campaign plans which identify governance and development programs that have considerable *relative advantages* to the people and tailor messages about programs to highlight those advantages will generate more rapid adoption and diffusion throughout the populace.

One of the most important things planners must do when implementing governance and development plans is to understand the context or the social system in which they are operate. Once

---

[105] Rogers, 106-118.

planners understand the social system they can assess if the programs they wish to implement are *compatible* with the culture. Webber stresses the importance of this approach when he highlights L.A. Brown's statement "suppliers of innovations have a role to play in encouraging their adoption – by adapting the innovation to the people's taste and pockets; by establishing agencies through which the innovation is distributed to the population and by encouraging its use."[106]

Making initiatives seem less *complex* is closely related to *compatibility* and the *communication channel*. If planners tailor messages to fit into the culture and utilize indigenous opinion leaders to communicate information about the innovations, they will seem less complex. There is less chance for misunderstandings, no need to translate information about the innovation. The opinion leader can place information about the innovation in the proper cultural context making it easier for people to understand and therefore increasing potential for adoption.

Planners should focus development efforts on initiatives which can be easily sampled by the local populace without a full commitment. The greater the risk to the individual, the less *tryable* the innovation is. If planners can implement programs on a trial basis to allow the population to experiment with the innovation and test it to experience its benefits first hand, adoption should increase. The analysis of alternative crop initiatives demonstrates these initiatives are not easily *tryable*. A possible technique to promote increased and more rapid adoption might be using the same method the insurgents use to encourage poppy cultivation. The USG could front the farmer the money and supplies to get the desired product started therefore reducing the risk and demonstrating greater *trialability*. Perhaps the most significant obstacle to any perceptions of *trialability* is the security situation. As long as people fear attacks from insurgents for trying new USG and Host Nation government sponsored programs, they will be less likely to adopt these innovations. Therefore, security must come first.

Making governance and development initiatives more observable to the populace requires a host nation face on everything. Host nation officials promoting development projects allow the population to

---

[106] Webber, 487.

observe their government in action. Locals *observing* host nation army and police actively patrolling and effectively protecting the population builds their trust and confidence and demonstrates the advantage of new systems and institutions. Operational commanders demonstrate this through partnered patrols with host nation forces in the lead. However, for these observations to lead to increased adoption, they must demonstrate positive results. Corruption could be the biggest obstacle to this. Observances of bad governance and corruption can have the exact opposite effect. Operational commanders must promote through mentorship professional, ethical host nation armed forces.

This is not to say that the USG in Afghanistan is not already employing many of the suggestions mentioned above. In fact, the USG has come a considerably long way in the right direction with regard to these needs. The HTT, PRT and ADT are all examples of organizations that did not exist in 2002 when the United States initially invaded Afghanistan. These organizations were born out of an identified need. While the leaders who instituted these organizations may not have read Rogers, or knew of diffusion of innovations, it is apparent that they recognized many of the same social phenomena at work in Afghanistan that diffusion researchers have identified and examined over the years. Therefore is it most important that the USG not lose the institutional knowledge it has gained over the last ten years of war.

Conclusion

This study demonstrates that many of these lessons conform to the elements of diffusion of innovations. The USG has developed HTTs to understand the culture in which it operates recognizing the importance of the social system's effects on the adoption of new ideas. While the HTTs are indispensable in helping operational commanders understand the culture and tailor programs for success, the USG must understand that the Afghan culture presents many obstacles to complete adoption of many desired programs and the potential for the Afghan people to reinvent innovations in undesirable ways is great. The development of the ADT to diffuse new agricultural innovations and techniques to the Afghan people is generally a positive trend. Aspects of the ADT's practices include designing agricultural development programs which best achieve the needs of the people. However, the ADTs and alternative agricultural development programs in Afghanistan face an uphill battle against the vastly more lucrative poppy trade. This study demonstrates that diffusion of innovations offers a particularly useful lens for understanding why Afghans are not adopting many of these agricultural development programs. Specifically because they do not demonstrate a *relative advantage* over poppy cultivation and it is hard for Afghans to try the new crops without losing considerable profits. Finally, the USG's fielding of PRTs has improved governance initiatives in the country. The PRTs consult local government officials ensuring governance has a constant Afghan face demonstrating Rogers' recommendation to enlist opinion leaders to help with the diffusion process and increase adoption potential. The PRT's consultation with local officials also ensures development programs meet the needs of the people demonstrating the new form of governance presents a *relative advantage* over the old form and is observable to the Afghan people. The PRTs and Brigades utilize radio to disseminate information about development initiatives because they understand that radio is one of the most important communication channels in Afghanistan.

This study demonstrates the power that diffusion of innovations can have in the examination of governance and development efforts in stability and support operations but more research is required to strengthen this line of thought. A comprehensive research agenda is required to learn the most we can about effective governance and development initiatives.[107] Future research should focus on specific programs designed with diffusion of innovations concepts in mind. Such research could utilize a quasi-experimental design where two groups are tested using different variables of diffusion research. A research study such as this could definitively prove the merits of diffusion of innovations ideas in USG stability and support operations. Once researchers can further demonstrate the efficacy of applying diffusion of innovations theory to USG governance and development efforts, then those tenets can be included into doctrine.

---

[107] Although this study brings many important lessons to light, it has limitations. The first shortfall is in its methods. Due to the limited scope, access, and time, the study is not an experimental quantitative research study. Its reliance on already existing data available in unclassified formats meant that the data is not ideal for the study of diffusion of innovations. The data available is too general and does not examine specific USG governance and development programs.

BIBLIOGRAPHY

Anonymous. "Social Science Teams Aid Army in Afghanistan." *Army Magazine*, 2007: 73-76.

Audit of USAID Afghanistan's Local Governance and Community Development Project in Southern and Eastern Regions of Afghainistan. Manila: Office of the Inspector General, USAID, 2009.

Brown, Lawrence A. *Innovation Diffusion: A New Perspective.* New York, NY: Methuen & Co., 1981.

Carden, Michael J. "Narcotics Trade Fuels Afghanistan Insurgency, Mullen Says." *American Forces Press Service*, Sepetember 19, 2008.

Chronology: The Evolution of the Bush Doctrine. Public Broadasting Service. n.d. http://www.pbs.org/wgbh/pages/frontline/shows/iraq/etc/cron.html (accessed February 28, 2012).

Cialdini, Robert B. *Influence: Science and Practice.* 4th ed. Needham Heights, MA: Allyn and Bacon, 2001.

Denoeux, Guilian, and Lynn Carter. "Development Assistance and Extemism: A Guide to Programing." Washington, DC: USAID, 2009.

Department of the Army. Field Manual 3-07, *Stability and Support Operations* 2008. Washington, DC: Government Printing Office, 2008.

Dessaso, Lieutenant Colonel Christopher D. "Towards Development of Afghanistan National Stability; Analysis in Historical, Military and Cultural Contexts." *SAMS Mongraph Series - Population Centric Counterinsurgency: A False Idol?* Edited by Dan G Cox, & Thomas Bruscino. Fort Leavenworth, KS: Combat Studies Institute Press, 2011. 63-98.

Emadi, Hafizullah. *Culture and Customs of Afghanistan.* Westport, CT: Greenwood Press, 2005.

Finney, Captain Nathan K. "Human Terrain Support for Current Operations." *Infantry Magazine*, March-June 2009: 4-6.

International Security Assistance Force. *International Security Assistance Force, Afghanistan* "About ISAF." http://www.isaf.nato.int/mission.html (accessed October 25, 2010).

Johnson, Charles M. "USAID Continues to Face Challenges in Managing and Overseeing U.S. Development Assistance Programs." Congressional Testimony, Washington DC: United States Government Accountability Office (July 2010). http://www.gao.gov/new.items/d10932t.pdf (accessed December 28, 2011).

Johnson, Gregory, Vijaya Ramachandran, and Julie Walz,. "The Commander's Emergency Response Program in Afghanistan: Five Practical Recommendations." *Center for Global Development.* n.d. http://www.cgdev.org/files/1425413_file_Johnson_Ramachandran_Walz_CERP_brief.pdf (accessed December 28, 2011).

Katzman, Kenneth. *Afghanistan: Politics, Elections and Government Performance.* Report to Congress, Washington DC: Congressional Research Service, 2011.

Katzman, Kenneth. *Afghanistan: Post Taliban Governance, Security and U.S. Policy.* Report to Congress, Washignton DC: Congressional Research Service, 2011.

Katzman, Kenneth. *Afghanistan:Current Issues and U.S. Policy Concerns.* Congressional, Washington DC: Congressional Research Service, Library of Congress, 2001.

Khadduri, Majid. *War and Peace in the Law of Islam.* Baltimore, MD: Johns Hopkins University Press, 2008.

MacVaugh, Jason, and Francesco Schiavone. "Limits to the Diffusion of Innovation: A Literature Review and Integrative Model." *European Journal of Innovation Management* 13, no. 2 (210): 197-221.

Malevich, Lieutenant Colonel John J. and Daryl C. Youngman. "The Afghan Balance of Power and the Culture of Jihad." *Military Review*, May/June 2011: 33-39.

Michaels, Jim. "In Afghanistan Fighting a Legacy of Corruption; It's a Way of Life -- and Hinders U.S. Efforts There." *USA Today*, November 23, 2009: A1.

Nyrop, Richard F. and Donald M. Seekins, ed. *Afghanistan: A Country Study.* 5th . Washington , DC: United States Government, 1986.

Perito, Robert M. *The U.S. Experience with Provincial Reconstruction Teams in Afghanistan Lessons Identified* . Special Report, Washington DC: United States Institute of Peace, n.d.

Rogers, Everett M, and F. Floyd Shoemaker. *Communication of Innovations: A Cross-Cultural Approach.* New York, NY: The Free Press, 1971.

Rogers, Everett M. *Diffusion of Innovations.* 5th. New York, NY: The Free Press, 2003.

Saikal, Amin. *Modern Afghanistan: A History of Struggle and Survival.* London: I. B. Tauris & Company Ltd., 2004.

Sherman, Lorraine. *Sustainability of US Government Projects in Afghanistan.* School of Advanced Military Studies, Command and General Staff College, Fort Leavenworth, KS: US Army Command and General Staff College, 2011.

Tariq, Mohammad Osman, Najla Ayoubi, Fazel Habi Haqbeen. *Afghanistan in 2010: A Survey of the Afghan People.* Survey, Kabul, Afghnistan: The Asia Foundation, 2010.

"The National Security Strategy of the United States." Washington DC: The White House, September 2002.

Turner, Rondal L. "Agricultural Development Teams and the Counterinsurgency in Afghanistan." *US Army War College Research Project.* Carlisle, PA: US Army War College, 2010.

United Nations. *UNICEF website.* http://www.unicef.org/infobycountry/afghanistan_statistics.html (accessed January 10, 2011).

Walker, J. "The Diffusion of Innovatoins Among States." *The Political Science Review* 63 (1969): 880-889.

Webber, Michael. "Classics in Human Geography Revisited: Brown, L. A. Innovation Diffusion: A New Perspective. London: Methuen, Commentary 1." *Progess in Human Geography*, 2006: 487-494.

Wellen, Russ. "Why Don't Iraqis and Afghans Embrace Democracy?" *Foreign Policy in Focus*, September 2010: 3.

Weusthuis, Martin. *Afghan Pomegranates in the Netherlands: Designing an International Pomegranate Supply Chain.* Thesis, Van Hall Larstein Universtiy of Applied Sciences, Wageningen, The Netherlands: Van Hall Larstein Universtiy of Applied Sciences, 2009.

www.ingramcontent.com/pod-product-compliance
Lightning Source LLC
Chambersburg PA
CBHW080635290526
45790CB00007B/3069

9781503305182